SUSTAINABLE ENGINEERING

BASIC CONCEPTS

Dr. Akshay Gupta

Dr. Chandra Prakash Gour

Dr. Anulipi Agrawal

Er. Aaisha Sayyed

SUSTAINABLE ENGINEERING – BASIC CONCEPTS

This book is dedicated to the students, engineers, and innovators who always lead the way toward a more sustainable and resilient world.

Contents

Foreword

Sustainability is no longer a choice, rather, it is a necessity. In an era marked by rapid urbanization, climate change, and the depletion of natural resources, the role of engineering must evolve to address global challenges responsibly and innovatively. This book, Sustainable Engineering, arrives at a critical moment, offering valuable insights into how engineering practices can be reimagined to align with environmental stewardship, economic viability, and social equity.

What distinguishes this book is its holistic approach. It does not treat sustainability as an isolated concept, but rather as a foundational principle embedded across the lifecycle of engineering design, construction, operation, and decommissioning. The author thoughtfully bridges theory and practice, combining established frameworks with current case studies, life cycle assessment methodologies, and green technology applications.

For students, this book serves as a gateway into a new paradigm of engineering thinking—one that prioritizes long-term impacts and responsible innovation. For professionals, it offers practical tools and perspectives that are increasingly demanded in global markets and policy frameworks. And for educators, it provides a solid foundation to shape the next generation of engineers committed to sustainability

I commend the author for contributing such a timely and relevant work to the academic and professional community. It is my sincere hope that this book will inspire readers to adopt sustainable principles not only in their engineering practices but also in their worldview.

Dr. Akshay Gupta

Dr. Chandra Prakash Gour

Dr. Anulipi Agrawal

Er. Aaisha Sayyed

Preface

The concept of sustainability has transitioned from a noble ideal to an urgent global imperative. As engineers, we stand at the forefront of designing systems, structures, and solutions that directly shape the quality of life and the health of our planet. Recognizing this responsibility, Sustainable Engineering was written to provide a comprehensive foundation for understanding and applying sustainable principles across engineering disciplines.

This book emerged from years of academic exploration, classroom teaching, and practical engagement with real-world challenges. It is designed for students, educators, and professionals who seek to integrate environmental, economic, and social considerations into their engineering decisions.

The chapters cover a wide range of topics, from sustainability fundamentals and green design principles to life cycle assessment, renewable energy technologies, sustainable construction practices, and emerging innovations. The content is supported by case studies, diagrams, and practical examples that aim to bridge theory and application. Each chapter concludes with key takeaways and reflective questions to promote critical thinking and deeper learning.

Writing this book has been both a professional and personal journey. It has reinforced my belief that sustainable engineering is not just a technical pursuit, but a moral commitment to future generations. We are deeply grateful to GH Raisoni College of Engineering and Management for their institutional support, and to our colleagues, students, and family who have encouraged me throughout this endeavor.

It is our hope that this book will inspire its readers to embrace sustainability not as a constraint, but as a powerful design opportunity, one that leads to resilient communities, responsible industries, and a healthier planet.

Dr. Akshay Gupta

Dr. Chandra Prakash Gour

Dr. Anulipi Agrawal

Er. Aaisha Sayyed

Acknowledgments

The journey of creating this book on Sustainable Engineering has been both intellectually rewarding and deeply inspiring. We would like to express our heartfelt gratitude to all those who contributed to its completion.

First and foremost, we extend our sincere thanks to the mentors and colleagues whose expertise and encouragement guided us throughout this endeavour. Their critical insights and unwavering support were instrumental in shaping the content and direction of this work.

We are especially thankful to GH Raisoni College of Engineering and Management, Jalgaon, for providing continuous support, academic resources, and an encouraging environment that greatly facilitated the development of this book.

We are also deeply grateful to the academic institutions and research centres that provided access to valuable resources, data, and case studies that enriched the depth of this book. Special thanks to Notion Press for their professionalism and commitment to quality.

To the many researchers, engineers, environmental scientists, and policymakers whose work has been referenced and built upon in this book, thank you for your contributions to the field of sustainable development.

We owe a special debt of appreciation to our families and friends for their patience, motivation, and emotional support throughout the writing process. Their belief in the importance of this work gave us strength and purpose.

Lastly, we dedicate this book to future engineers and innovators who are committed to building a more sustainable, equitable, and resilient world.

Warm Regards

Dr. Akshay Gupta

Dr. Chandra Prakash Gour

Dr. Anulipi Agrawal

Er. Aaisha Sayyed

Prologue/Introduction

In the age of accelerating climate change, resource depletion, and urban expansion, the need for sustainable thinking in every sphere of human activity has never been greater. Engineering, as a discipline that transforms ideas into tangible reality, holds the unique power and responsibility, to drive that change.

This book, Sustainable Engineering, was born from a deep conviction: that engineering solutions must no longer be judged solely by their technical efficiency or economic viability, but by their long-term impact on people and the planet. The traditional paradigms of design, construction, and manufacturing must evolve to prioritize resilience, circularity, and ecological harmony.

The prologue to any story sets the tone for what lies ahead. Likewise, this book opens with a call, not just for innovation, but for introspection. It challenges students, professionals, educators, and policymakers to rethink the values that underpin engineering decisions. It invites them to view sustainability not as a constraint but as a creative framework for developing smarter, cleaner, and more inclusive solutions.

Through interdisciplinary insights, real-world case studies, and practical tools, this book seeks to empower readers to become catalysts for sustainable transformation. Whether designing infrastructure, developing materials, or leading projects, engineers can be architects of a future that balances progress with preservation.

As you begin this journey through the principles and practices of sustainable engineering, I invite you to consider your role in shaping a future where development and sustainability are not at odds, but in harmony.

1. Life Cycle Assessment

Overview

Sustainable engineering, as a discipline, seeks to address the pressing need to balance technological development with environmental responsibility. In a world marked by rapid industrialization, population growth, and resource depletion, engineers must adopt tools and methodologies that allow for a comprehensive evaluation of the environmental implications of their designs and decisions. One such critical tool is the Life Cycle Assessment (LCA), a methodology that provides a systemic perspective on the environmental impacts of a product, process, or service across its entire life span, i.e., from raw material extraction to final disposal.

The concept of LCA is grounded in the principle that all products and processes consume resources and generate emissions throughout their lifecycle. These stages typically include raw material acquisition, manufacturing, transportation, usage, and end-of-life treatment such as recycling or disposal. By evaluating each stage quantitatively, LCA helps identify opportunities to reduce environmental impacts, optimize resource usage, and make informed choices that support sustainability. The growing emphasis on sustainable practices in industry, policy, and academia has made LCA an indispensable tool in the field of environmental engineering and sustainable development.

Phases of LCA

LCA is standardized by the International Organization for Standardization (ISO), particularly in ISO 14040 and ISO 14044, which outline a four-phase framework. All the phases of LCA are illustrated in Figure 1.1.

The first phase is the goal and scope definition, where the purpose of the study is clearly stated, and boundaries are established. The functional unit, a key concept in LCA, is defined in this phase. It represents a quantified reference against which inputs and outputs are normalized. For instance, if the LCA is evaluating two types of packaging, the functional unit might be "one Liter of liquid packaged and delivered to the consumer." The system boundaries determine which processes are included, such as whether the analysis considers only manufacturing and use phases, or includes raw material extraction and disposal as well.

The second phase is the life cycle inventory (LCI). This involves the collection of data regarding all the energy and material inputs and environmental emissions associated with each process in the system. This phase is often the most data-intensive, requiring detailed information on raw material usage, energy consumption, emissions to air, water, and land, and waste generation. Data may be obtained from direct measurements, published databases, industrial reports, or estimations, depending on the availability and reliability of sources.

Following the inventory is the life cycle impact assessment (LCIA). This phase translates the inventory data into potential environmental impacts. For example, carbon dioxide emissions contribute to global warming potential, while nitrogen oxides and sulphur dioxide may contribute to acidification. The LCIA process typically includes classification (assigning inventory flows to impact categories), characterization (quantifying the contribution of each flow to its impact), and, optionally, normalization and weighting (to compare and rank impacts). The objective of LCIA is to provide a clearer understanding of how different emissions and resource uses affect environmental issues such as climate change, resource depletion, ecosystem degradation, and human health.

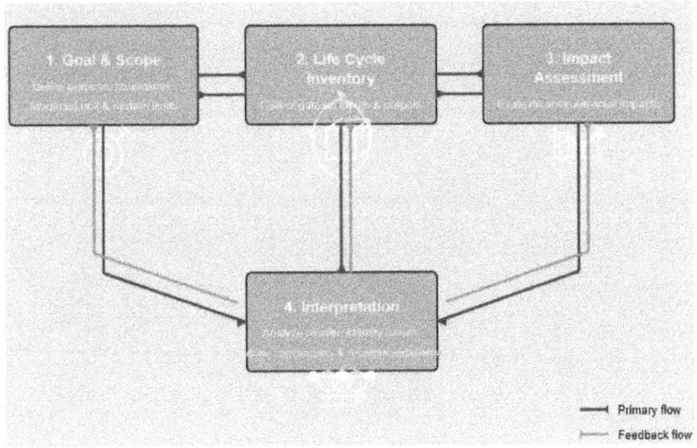

Figure 1.1: Phases of LCA

The final phase of an LCA is interpretation, where the results of the inventory and impact assessment are analysed with the original goal and scope. This phase is crucial for drawing meaningful conclusions and making recommendations. It involves evaluating the completeness, consistency, and sensitivity of the study and identifying the most significant environmental issues, which are often referred to as "hotspots" that drive the overall impacts. Based on this, strategies for improvement can be proposed, such as changes in material choice, process optimization, or increased recycling.

Applications of LCA

Life Cycle Assessment finds application across a broad spectrum of industries and policy domains. It is extensively used in product development to compare design alternatives and select options with the lowest environmental burden. It aids policymakers in formulating environmental regulations and sustainable procurement guidelines. Companies utilize LCA to support eco-labelling, environmental declarations, and corporate sustainability reporting.

Moreover, LCA is integral to green building certifications, sustainable supply chain management, and circular economy strategies. As environmental awareness grows among consumers and stakeholders, LCA provides the scientific basis to substantiate environmental claims and drive innovation.

Dr. Akshay Gupta, Dr. Chandra Prakash Gour, Dr. Anulipi Agrawal,
Er. Aaisha Sayyed

Types of LCA

There are primarily two types of LCA, i.e., attributional and consequential. Attributional LCA focuses on describing the environmental properties of a product as it is currently produced, without considering broader systemic changes. This is useful for benchmarking and environmental labelling. In contrast, consequential LCA evaluates the environmental consequences of a change in the system, such as switching from fossil fuels to biofuels, including market and behavioural responses. Each type has its merits and is selected based on the specific goal of the assessment. The different types of LCA are mentioned in Figure 1.2. Table 1.1 shows the comparison of both attributional and consequential LCA.

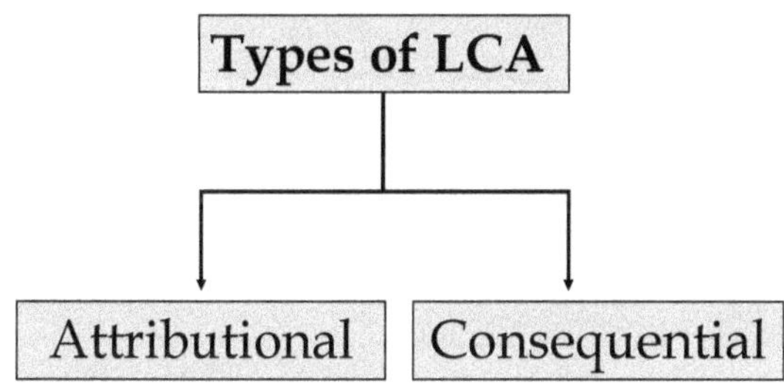

Figure 1.2: Types of LCA

Challenges and Limitations

Despite its advantages, LCA is not without challenges. One major limitation is the availability and quality of data. Inaccurate or outdated data can lead to misleading results. Moreover, setting appropriate system boundaries and assumptions can be complex and subjective, potentially influencing the outcome significantly. LCA is also resource and time-intensive, which may limit its feasibility for small-scale or time-sensitive projects. Additionally, interpreting the results requires careful consideration, particularly when weighing impacts that affect diverse environmental endpoints. The main challenges and limitations that are mainly faced are mentioned in Figure 1.3.

Table 1.1: Comparison Between Attributional and Consequential LCA

Aspect	Attributional LCA	Consequential LCA
Definition	Describes the environmental impacts of a product or system as it exists.	Evaluates the environmental consequences of changes in a system or decisions.
Scope	Static — focuses on average data and existing conditions.	Dynamic — considers market-driven effects and system-wide changes.
Purpose	Used for reporting, benchmarking, and certification.	Used for policy-making, strategic planning, and evaluating future scenarios.
Data Type	Uses average or historical data.	Uses marginal data (i.e., data representing changes due to decisions).

Practical Examples Related to LCA

A cradle-to-grave approach in LCA assesses the environmental impacts of a product or system across its entire life cycle, starting from the extraction of raw materials

Dr. Akshay Gupta, Dr. Chandra Prakash Gour, Dr. Anulipi Agrawal,
Er. Aaisha Sayyed

(cradle), through manufacturing, use, and finally to disposal or end-of-life (grave). However, the cradle-to-cradle approach extends the LCA concept beyond disposal by integrating product reuse, recycling, or upcycling at the end of life. It envisions a closed-loop system, where materials re-enter the production cycle, mimicking natural processes in which "waste" becomes a resource. To illustrate its practical utility, consider the comparison between conventional internal combustion engine vehicles and electric vehicles. Electric vehicles have zero tailpipe emissions, but their life cycle impacts must account for electricity generation, battery production, and end-of-life management. A typical example of the product lifecycle is shown in Figure 1.4, which begins with the extraction of the raw materials and ends with the treatment of the waste.

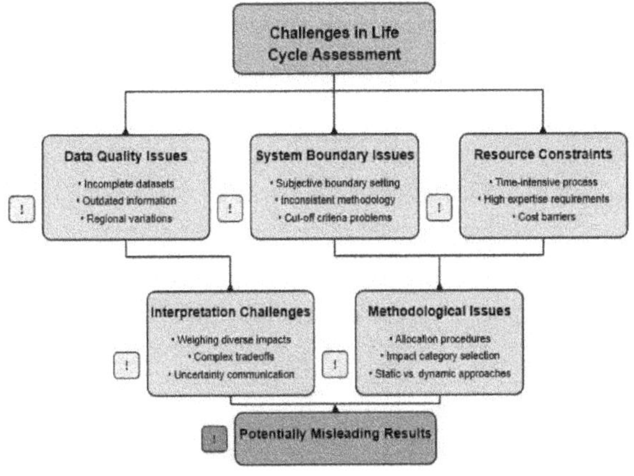

Figure 1.3: Challenges and Limitations of LCA

An LCA reveals that although electric vehicles can have lower overall greenhouse gas emissions over their life span, their

7

manufacturing stage, particularly battery production, has a higher environmental footprint. This insight is crucial in guiding design improvements, such as enhancing battery efficiency and sourcing cleaner electricity. The differences between cradle to grave and cradle to cradle are given in Table 1.2.

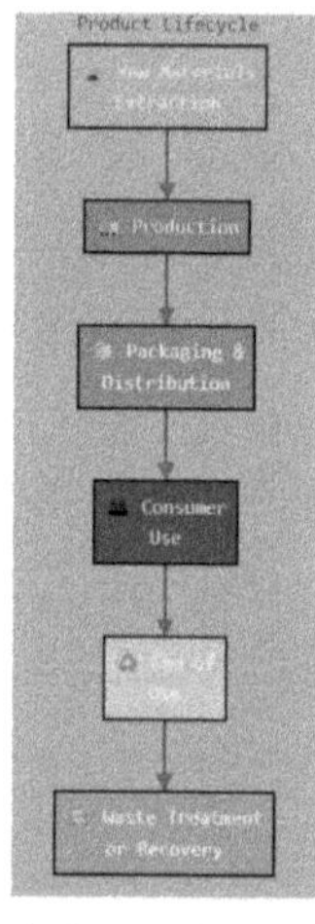

Figure 1.4: Typical example of a product lifecycle

In conclusion, Life Cycle Assessment is a foundational tool in sustainable engineering, enabling a comprehensive and scientifically robust evaluation of environmental impacts. By promoting transparency and informed decision-making, LCA empowers engineers, designers, and policymakers to move beyond incremental improvements and towards truly sustainable solutions. In the chapters that follow, we will explore how LCA integrates with other sustainability principles and how it is applied in specific sectors like construction, energy, and water management to drive a more resilient and responsible engineering practice.

Table 1.2: Difference between cradle to grave and cradle to cradle

Feature	Cradle-to-Grave	Cradle-to-Cradle
End-of-Life Perspective	Treated as final disposal (landfill/incineration)	Treated as a resource for reuse or recycling
Design Approach	Often linear—focus on minimizing impact	Circular—focus on eliminating waste and reuse
Resource Use	One-time extraction and use	Continuous reuse in closed loops
Sustainability Contribution	Identifies impact hotspots for improvement	Promotes regenerative, circular systems
Product Example	Disposable plastic utensils	Modular electronics are designed for disassembly

Life Cycle Thinking and Pollution Prevention

Life cycle thinking extends the concept of pollution prevention beyond immediate environmental impacts to encompass the entire product life cycle. This holistic perspective promotes sustainability by emphasizing the reduction of environmental burdens at every stage, i.e., from raw material extraction to end-of-life disposal. Within this context, source reduction aligns closely with the principles of eco-design and is encapsulated by what is commonly referred to as the "6 RE Philosophy." This approach advocates for the following strategies:

Re-think: Evaluate the product and its intended functions critically. By optimizing the design and utility of the product, it is possible to reduce the consumption of energy and natural resources significantly.

Re-duce: Minimize the usage of energy and raw materials throughout the product's life cycle, thereby lowering environmental impact and resource depletion.

Re-place: Substitute hazardous or non-renewable substances with more environmentally benign and sustainable alternatives during the product development process.

Re-cycle: Prioritize the use of recyclable materials in product design. Additionally, structure the product to facilitate easy disassembly, thereby enhancing its potential for recycling at the end of its useful life.

Re-use: Design products in a modular fashion that allows for components or entire assemblies to be reused, extending their lifecycle and reducing the need for new resource inputs.

Re-pair: Ensure the product can be easily repaired, thereby postponing the need for replacement and reducing the generation of waste.

Summary and Conclusion

This chapter introduced the concept of Life Cycle Assessment (LCA) as a vital tool in the practice of sustainable engineering.

Dr. Akshay Gupta, Dr. Chandra Prakash Gour, Dr. Anulipi Agrawal,
Er. Aaisha Sayyed

LCA provides a systematic framework for evaluating the environmental impacts associated with every stage of a product or process life cycle—from raw material extraction, manufacturing, and use, to final disposal. It is structured into four key phases: goal and scope definition, life cycle inventory (LCI), life cycle impact assessment (LCIA), and interpretation. The chapter discussed how LCA supports informed decision-making by identifying environmental "hotspots" and enabling comparison of alternatives. It also highlighted the applications of LCA in various industries, the distinction between attributional and consequential approaches, and the limitations associated with data availability, boundary setting, and interpretation.

Life Cycle Assessment serves as the cornerstone of environmentally responsible engineering. By shifting the focus from localized impacts to a comprehensive, cradle-to-grave perspective, LCA enables engineers and stakeholders to understand the true environmental cost of products and processes. As global sustainability challenges intensify, incorporating LCA into design, policy, and innovation is no longer optional; rather, it is essential. This chapter lays the groundwork for applying LCA as both a decision-support tool and a driver of sustainable transformation across engineering domains.

Exercises

Q. 1: Explain the four main phases of a Life Cycle Assessment (LCA) as defined by ISO 14040. Why is each phase important in understanding the environmental impact of a product?

Q. 2: Compare and contrast Attributional and Consequential LCA. Provide examples where each type would be appropriately applied.

Q. 3: What is meant by a 'functional unit' in LCA? Illustrate with a practical example how the choice of a functional unit can influence the outcomes of an assessment.

Q. 4: Describe the concept of cradle-to-grave and cradle-to-cradle assessments in LCA. How do these approaches differ in their contribution to sustainable engineering?

Q. 5: Discuss the potential challenges and limitations faced while conducting an LCA study. How can these limitations be minimized or addressed?

Q. 6: How can LCA be used as a tool for environmental decision-making in product design and development? Provide a real-world example.

Q. 7: Illustrate the lifecycle of a typical consumer product (e.g., a plastic bottle or smartphone) using the material flow perspective. Discuss key stages that contribute most to environmental impacts.

Q. 8: How does Life Cycle Assessment support the goals of sustainable development and circular economy?

Q. 9: Explain the 6RE philosophy in detail.

2. Risk Assessment

Overview

Risk assessment is a critical process in sustainable engineering, enabling engineers and environmental professionals to evaluate the likelihood and severity of adverse effects resulting from exposure to environmental hazards. These hazards may arise from chemical contaminants, industrial processes, or natural events. The goal is to understand the severity of a risk, whether it is acceptable or requires intervention, and how best to prioritize resources for risk mitigation.

Risk, in simple terms, is the probability of an adverse outcome resulting from exposure to a hazardous agent. In environmental contexts, risk is often a function of hazard (the intrinsic potential of a substance to cause harm) and exposure (the extent to which a population or system comes in contact with the hazard). Figure 2.1 shows the flowchart explaining the risk and its potential factors in detail.

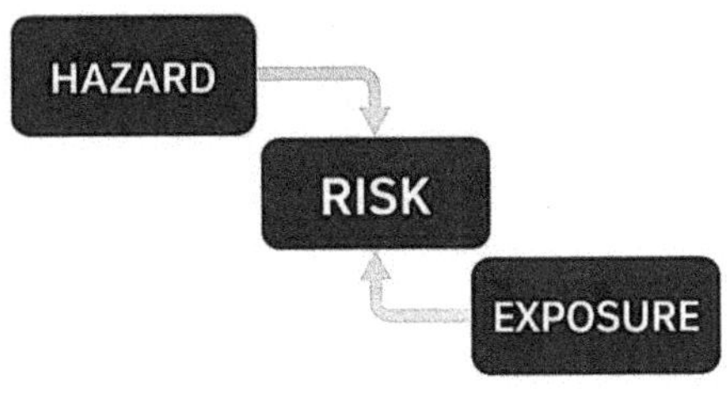

Figure 2.1: Components of Risk

Types of Risks in Environmental Contexts

Environmental risks can be grouped into three broad categories:

1. *Voluntary Exposure Risks*: These include risks willingly taken, such as smoking, mountain climbing, or skydiving.

2. *Involuntary Exposure Risks*: These arise from environmental pollution (e.g., air pollutants in urban areas or industrial zones) and are not under direct personal control.

3. *Natural Disaster Risks*: Earthquakes, floods, and other natural phenomena that present unpredictable and often uncontrollable threats.

In sustainable engineering, involuntary risks from chemical releases, waste management failures, and long-term pollutant exposure are of prime concern. Figure 2.2 shows the different types of risk present in the environment.

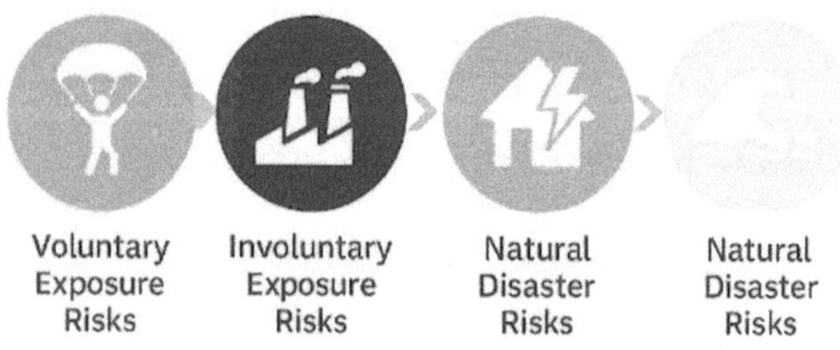

Figure 2.2: Types of Risks

Dr. Akshay Gupta, Dr. Chandra Prakash Gour, Dr. Anulipi Agrawal,
Er. Aaisha Sayyed

Risk Assessment Framework

Risk assessment involves a systematic approach to identify, evaluate, and quantify potential health and environmental risks. The standard steps are as follows:

a) Hazard Identification

This involves recognizing a chemical or process that may cause harm. The chemical's toxicity, persistence, and pathways into the human or ecological system are analysed.

b) Dose-Response Assessment

This step establishes the relationship between the extent of exposure and the severity of the effect. The concept of NOAEL (No Observed Adverse Effect Level) and LOAEL (Lowest Observed Adverse Effect Level) is crucial here. EC50 (Effective Concentration for 50% of the population) is often used for quantifying potency.

c) Exposure Assessment

Here, the pathway and magnitude of human or ecological exposure to the hazard are estimated. Factors such as duration, frequency, and routes of exposure (ingestion, inhalation, skin contact) are considered.

d) *Risk Characterization*

This step combines the information from the previous steps to estimate the risk, providing a comprehensive picture of the likelihood and severity of effects. Risk characterization leads to informed decision-making on whether a hazard poses an acceptable risk or requires mitigation.

2.4 Toxicology and Environmental Health

Toxicology, the study of the adverse effects of chemical, physical, or biological agents on living organisms, encompasses a range of critical terminologies that aid in the characterization and understanding of toxic substances and their effects. The following definitions are fundamental within the field:

- **Toxicant:** A synthetic or anthropogenic chemical substance that elicits toxic effects. These compounds are typically man-made and introduced into the environment through human activities.
- **Toxin:** A naturally occurring toxic substance that is biosynthesized by living organisms, including plants, animals, bacteria, or fungi.
- **Acute Exposure:** A single or short-term exposure to a toxic substance, typically resulting in immediate or rapid onset of toxic effects.

- **Chronic Exposure:** Prolonged or repeated exposure to a toxicant or toxin over an extended period, often resulting in delayed or cumulative health effects.

- **Latency:** The time interval between initial exposure to a toxic substance and the manifestation of observable adverse effects or symptoms.

The dose-response curve illustrates how different concentrations or durations of exposure relate to observed health effects, forming the foundation for regulatory standards, as shown in Figure 2.3.

Carcinogenic vs. Non-Carcinogenic Risk

- **Carcinogens:** These substances cause or promote cancer. Regulatory standards aim for risk levels as low as "1 in a million".

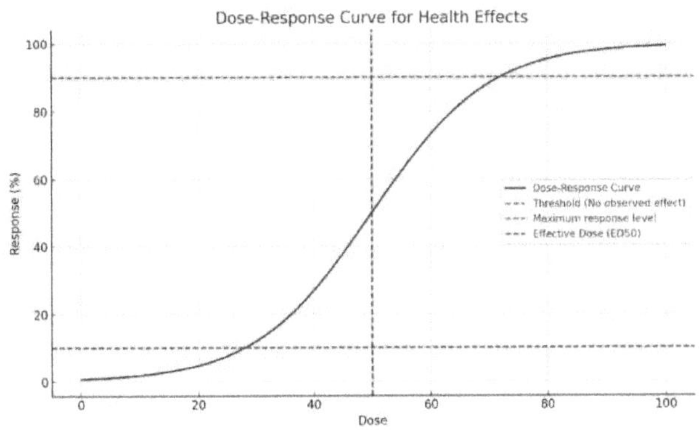

Figure 2.3: Dose Response Curve for Health Effects

- **Non-Carcinogens**: Substances that affect other organ systems (e.g., lead impacting the nervous system or boron affecting reproductive health).

The basic difference between Carcinogenic and Non-Carcinogenic risk is illustrated through a pictorial representation as shown in Figure 2.4.

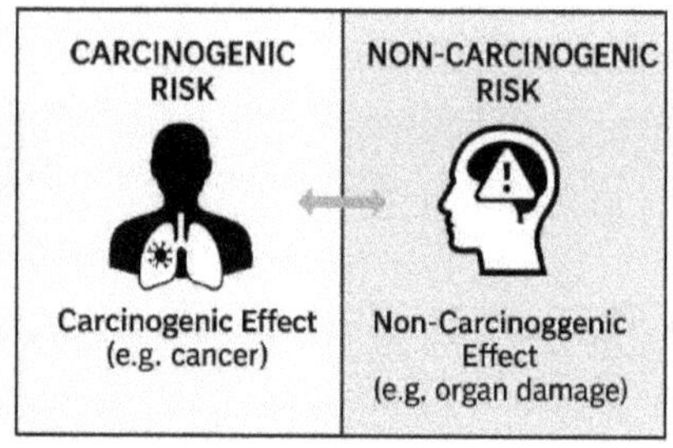

Figure 2.4: Carcinogenic and non-carcinogenic risk

Bioavailability and Bioaccumulation

Bioavailability refers to the fraction of a contaminant that is accessible to organisms for absorption. A contaminant may be present in the environment but not bioavailable, reducing its immediate risk. However, environmental changes (e.g., pH, oxygen level) can make these compounds bioavailable over time.

Bioaccumulation, on the other hand, refers to the buildup of substances like mercury in organisms over time, often increasing in concentration up the food chain and posing significant ecological and health threats. The pictorial

Dr. Akshay Gupta, Dr. Chandra Prakash Gour, Dr. Anulipi Agrawal, Er. Aaisha Sayyed

representation of bioavailability and bioaccumulation is shown in Figure 2.5.

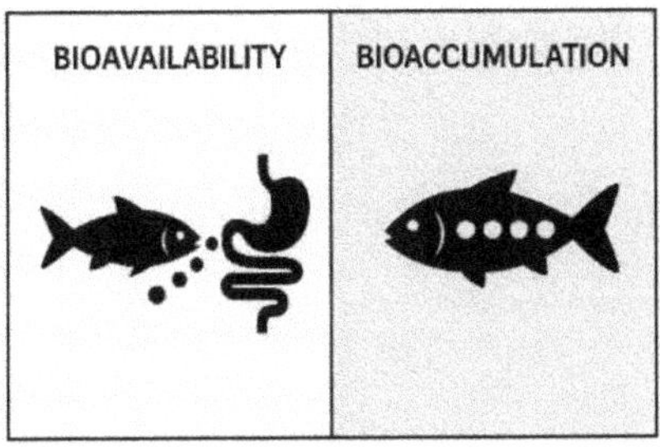

Figure 2.5: Bioavailability and Bioaccumulation

Persistent Organic Pollutants and Case Examples

Some chemicals, like PCBs (Polychlorinated Biphenyls) and dioxins, are classified as Persistent Organic Pollutants (POPs). These are resistant to environmental degradation, bioaccumulate, and can travel long distances through air or water.

For instance:

- **PCBs** have been linked to endocrine disruption and reproductive toxicity.

- **Dioxins**, produced during waste burning, are potent carcinogens and immunosuppressants. High-profile contamination incidents (e.g., Hudson River PCB cleanup or dioxin poisoning of Viktor Yushchenko) highlight their seriousness.

Environmental Modelling and Site Assessment

Effective risk assessment often relies on environmental models that simulate contaminant transport and fate. These models incorporate physical (advection, diffusion), chemical (sorption, degradation), and biological (uptake, transformation) processes. Site-specific studies, supported by lab data and monitoring, guide remediation efforts.

Importance of Quantitative Measurements

Quantitative measurement plays a vital role in environmental risk assessment and sustainable engineering practices. By quantifying contaminant concentrations, typically expressed in units such as milligrams per Liter (mg/L) or micrograms per kilogram (µg/kg), engineers and environmental scientists can accurately define the severity of environmental problems. These precise measurements are fundamental in designing effective remediation systems tailored to the specific nature and concentration of pollutants present. Furthermore, quantification supports the establishment and enforcement of environmental standards that ensure public safety and ecological health. For example, regulatory benchmarks like the permissible arsenic level in drinking water, currently set at 10 µg/L, are the result of rigorous risk-based assessment processes. In addition to informing environmental compliance,

Dr. Akshay Gupta, Dr. Chandra Prakash Gour, Dr. Anulipi Agrawal,
Er. Aaisha Sayyed

quantitative data strengthens scientific research and provides a solid foundation for policy development, helping to ensure that interventions are both evidence-based and effective in mitigating environmental risks.

Conclusion

Risk assessment is a foundational component of sustainable engineering. It allows for a structured, scientific evaluation of hazards, enabling proactive management of environmental and health threats. With a blend of toxicology, environmental modelling, regulatory benchmarks, and site-specific analysis, risk assessment equips engineers to make informed decisions that safeguard both ecosystems and public health. As we move toward more complex and interconnected systems, risk assessment will continue to play a pivotal role in designing sustainable and resilient solutions.

Exercises

Q. 1: Define environmental risk and explain how it is calculated. What is the relationship between hazard and exposure?

Q. 2: Describe the four stages of the risk assessment framework. Illustrate each stage with a relevant environmental example.

Q. 3: Differentiate between carcinogenic and non-carcinogenic risks. Provide examples of substances that fall under each category.

Q. 4: Explain the significance of bioavailability and bioaccumulation in assessing environmental risks. Why are these concepts important in toxicology?

Q. 5: What are voluntary and involuntary risks in the context of environmental exposure? How should they be treated differently in risk management?

Q. 6: Using a dose-response curve, explain the terms NOAEL, LOAEL, and EC50. Why are these values crucial in setting regulatory standards?

Q. 7: How can risk assessment help in managing persistent organic pollutants (POPs)? Support your answer with an example.

Q. 8: What role does environmental modelling play in exposure assessment? Describe one situation where modelling is essential.

Q. 9: Explain in detail about Toxicology and Dose-Response Curve for Health Effects.

3. Environmental Data Collection and LCA Methodology

Introduction

In the field of sustainable engineering, accurate environmental data forms the backbone of informed decision-making. Whether designing water treatment systems, assessing waste management strategies, or conducting Life Cycle Assessments (LCA), reliable data is crucial. This chapter explores the systematic approach to environmental data collection, various analytical methods and instruments used, data quality assurance techniques, and how this information feeds into LCA methodology.

Importance of Environmental Data Collection

Environmental engineering tasks, such as evaluating pollutant concentrations, modelling emissions, or estimating environmental impacts, require high-quality data. Data that lacks precision or reliability can lead to flawed designs, over- or under-engineering, and ultimately unsustainable solutions. Thus, comprehensive data collection and stringent quality assurance (QA) and quality control (QC) measures are imperative. The important aspects of Environmental Data collections are shown in Figure 3.1.

Figure 3.1: Importance of Environmental Data Collection

Sampling and Sample Preparation

Physical Preparation

After sample collection, physical preparation enhances representativeness and improves analytical outcomes. Common steps include three different steps. The first step includes mixing of sample. This is done to homogenize the heterogeneous samples. This is followed by a drying and grinding process of the samples. This process is carried out to increase the surface area and the consistency. Finally, filtration or sieving of the sample is carried out, which is dependent on the type of analysis. The step-by-step sampling and physical preparation process is shown in Figure 3.2.

Dr. Akshay Gupta, Dr. Chandra Prakash Gour, Dr. Anulipi Agrawal,
Er. Aaisha Sayyed

Chemical Preparation

Chemical preparation often includes three different steps. All the steps of chemical preparation are described as follows:

1. Acid Digestion

Purpose:

To break down the organic matrix in environmental samples (e.g., soil, sludge, sediments) and release bound heavy metals (e.g., lead, cadmium, mercury) into solution for analysis.

Process:

- A known amount of sample is placed in a digestion vessel (usually a glass or Teflon beaker).

- Strong acids such as nitric acid (HNO_3), hydrochloric acid (HCl), or a combination including hydrofluoric acid (HF) and perchloric acid ($HClO_4$) are added.

- The sample is heated (often on a hot plate or in a microwave digester) until organic matter is oxidized and metals are released into the acid solution.

- After digestion, the resulting liquid is filtered (if needed) and analyzed using techniques like ICP-AES, ICP-MS, or AAS.

Applications:

- Determination of heavy metals in soil, sediments, wastewater sludges.

- Preparation of samples for regulatory compliance (e.g., TCLP testing for hazardous waste).

Cautions:

- Must be done under a fume hood due to toxic vapors.

- Requires careful handling and waste disposal because of corrosive and hazardous acids.

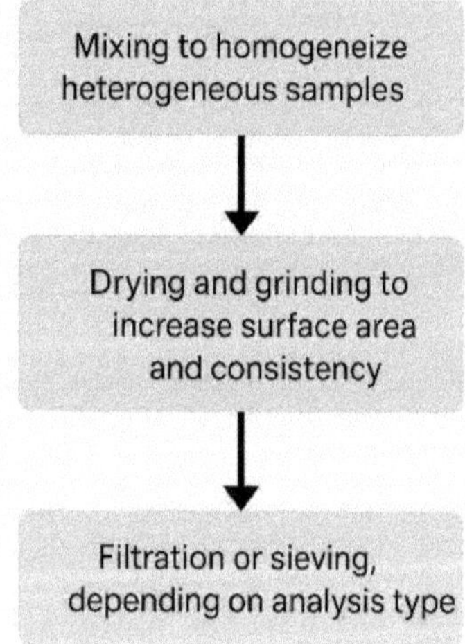

Figure 3.2: Physical preparation process and sampling

Dr. Akshay Gupta, Dr. Chandra Prakash Gour, Dr. Anulipi Agrawal,
Er. Aaisha Sayyed

2. Solvent Extraction

Purpose:

To extract organic contaminants (e.g., pesticides, PAHs, VOCs, PCBs) from aqueous or solid environmental samples using immiscible organic solvents.

Process:

- A known amount of the sample (solid or water) is mixed with an appropriate organic solvent (e.g., benzene, toluene, methylene chloride, hexane).

- The mixture is agitated or sonicated to allow the transfer of organic contaminants into the solvent layer.

- The solvent layer containing the contaminants is separated (often using a separatory funnel).

- The extract is concentrated (evaporated under nitrogen or vacuum) and cleaned up (using silica/alumina columns if needed).

- The final extract is analyzed using GC, GC-MS, or HPLC.

Applications:

- Measurement of organics like PAHs (polycyclic aromatic hydrocarbons), TCE (trichloroethylene), PCBs.

- Widely used in groundwater, wastewater, and contaminated soil analysis.

Cautions:

- Organic solvents are flammable and toxic; proper PPE and ventilation are mandatory.

- Solvent selection depends on analyte polarity and solubility.

3. Chemical Oxidation

Purpose: To break down complex organic molecules in environmental samples into simpler compounds, often as part of tests that measure oxidizable substances.

Process:

- The sample is reacted with a strong oxidizing agent, such as potassium dichromate ($K_2Cr_2O_7$), in the presence of sulfuric acid (H_2SO_4).

- The mixture is heated under reflux or digestion conditions for a specified period.

- The amount of oxidant consumed reflects the amount of oxidizable organic material in the sample.

- Commonly analyzed via titration (e.g., COD test) or spectrophotometry.

Applications:

- Determination of Chemical Oxygen Demand (COD) — A key parameter in water and wastewater treatment.

- Oxidation of organic matter for total organic carbon (TOC) analysis in environmental matrices.

Cautions:

- Strong oxidants are hazardous and corrosive.

- Chromium-based reagents are toxic and require careful disposal under hazardous waste protocols.

The summary of the Chemical preparation of the sample is given in Table 3.1.

Table 3.1: Summary of Chemical Analysis

Step	Purpose	Common Reagents	Typical Analysis Methods
Acid Digestion	Release metals from complex matrices	HNO_3, HCl, HF, $HClO_4$	ICP, AAS, ICP-MS
Solvent Extraction	Isolate organic pollutants from samples	Benzene, Toluene, DCM	GC, GC-MS, HPLC
Chemical Oxidation	Oxidize organics for parameter estimation	$K_2Cr_2O_7$, H_2SO_4	COD (Titration), TOC Analysis

Analytical Instruments and Techniques

Modern environmental labs employ a variety of analytical instruments based on the type of contaminant. The type of instruments includes a spectrophotometer, an Ion Chromatograph (IC), a Gas Chromatograph (GC), a GC-MS, an HPLC/LC-MS, an ICP-AES/ICP-MS, and an atomic absorption spectrometer (AAS). The target analyte and techniques for these instruments are given in Table 3.2.

Dr. Akshay Gupta, Dr. Chandra Prakash Gour, Dr. Anulipi Agrawal, Er. Aaisha Sayyed

Table 3.2: Analytical instruments and their techniques

Instrument	Target Analyte	Technique
Spectrophotometer	Various (e.g., COD, heavy metals)	Measures light absorbance at specific wavelengths.
Ion Chromatograph (IC)	Anions and cations	Separates ions by their charge and retention time.
Gas Chromatograph (GC)	Volatile organic compounds	Separates gases or liquids converted to gas.
GC-MS	Unknown organics	Identifies and quantifies based on mass-to-charge ratio.
HPLC / LC-MS	Large organics, pharmaceuticals	Analyzes complex liquid samples.
ICP-AES / ICP-MS	Heavy metals	Measures elemental concentration through atomic emission.
Atomic Absorption Spectrometer (AAS)	Single element analysis	Absorption of light by ground-state atoms.

Each of these instruments must be calibrated using standard solutions, and data is interpreted through calibration curves that correlate instrument response to known concentrations. It may be noticed that each instrument has its physical advantage based on the technique for which it is used.

Calibration and Quality Control

Calibration Curve

Instruments rely on calibration curves derived from standard solutions. The calibration must be checked regularly using the following checks:

- ***Calibration Check Samples:*** Known concentration samples not used in calibration.

- ***Blanks:*** To verify no contamination in reagents or glassware.

- ***Spiked Samples:*** To evaluate recovery and ensure matrix compatibility.

- ***Replicates:*** Multiple measurements of the same sample to assess reproducibility.

The calibration curves can be studied through a graphical image, as shown in Figure 3.3.

Dr. Akshay Gupta, Dr. Chandra Prakash Gour, Dr. Anulipi Agrawal,
Er. Aaisha Sayyed

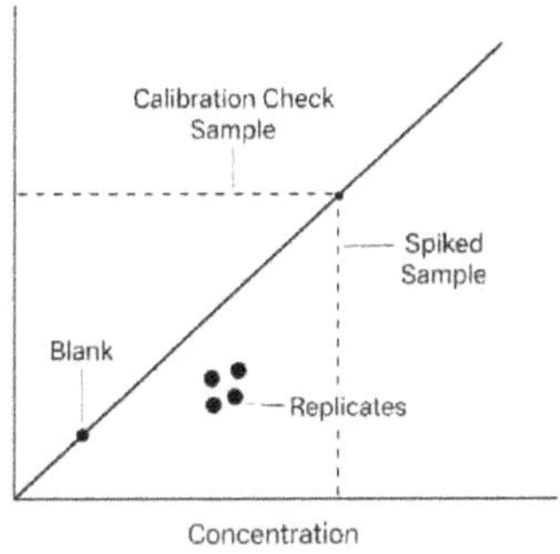

Figure 3.3: Calibration Curve

Method Detection Limit (MDL)

The MDL is the lowest concentration of an analyte that can be reliably distinguished from zero. It is calculated as:

$$\text{MDL} = t_{(n-1,\,99\%)} \times s$$

Where:

- t = t-distribution value at 99% confidence,

- s = standard deviation of replicate analyses.

The value of t can be analysed using the t-table (2-tailed, at 95% confidence). The t-table for the evaluation of the t value is given in Table 3.3 for the given degrees of freedom (d_f).

Consider an example of seven samples having arsenic values in micrograms per Liter. Assume the arsenic values of the samples as 0.98, 1.05, 1.01, 1.00, 1.02, 0.99, and 1.04, respectively. The value of the mean and the standard deviation can be calculated as follows:

Mean (μ):

$$\mu = \frac{0.98 + 1.05 + 1.01 + 1.00 + 1.02 + 0.99 + 1.04}{7} = \frac{7.09}{7} = 1.013\ \mu g/$$

Standard deviation (SD):

$$SD = \sqrt{\frac{\sum (x_i - \mu)^2}{n - 1}} \approx 0.025$$

Table 3.3: t-Table (Two-Tailed, 95% Confidence Level)

Degrees of Freedom (d_f)	t-value (95% confidence)
1	12.706
2	4.303
3	3.182
4	2.776
5	2.571
6	2.447
7	2.365
8	2.306
9	2.262
10	2.228
∞ (Z)	1.960

Dr. Akshay Gupta, Dr. Chandra Prakash Gour, Dr. Anulipi Agrawal,
Er. Aaisha Sayyed

Numerical Examples

Example 1: *You measured the concentration of arsenic (As) in a water sample using 7 replicates. The results (μg/L) are: 0.98, 1.05, 1.01, 1.00, 1.02, 0.99, 1.04*

Calculate the Method Detection Limit (MDL). (Use t value as 3.143)

Solution: *We have already calculated the values of mean and standard deviation for the same set in the previous section. Thus, let us start this numerical from Step 2.*

Step 1: Calculate the Standard Deviation (SD)

Discussed in the previous section.

Step 2: Apply the MDL Formula

$$\text{MDL} = t_{(n-1,\,99\%)} \times SD$$

- $n = 7$, degrees of freedom = 6

- $t_{(6,\,99\%)} \approx 3.143$ (from t-distribution table)

$$\text{MDL} = 3.143 \times 0.025 = 0.0786\,\mu g/L$$

Unsolved Example 2: *You ran 7 replicate measurements of a blank spiked with a low concentration of mercury (Hg) in recycled paper. The readings (in μg/g) were:*

0.031, 0.035, 0.032, 0.030, 0.033, 0.029, 0.034

Calculate the Method Detection Limit (MDL). (Use t value as 3.143)

Data Quality Assurance and Control (QA/QC)

The integrity of environmental engineering outcomes, whether in pollution control, resource recovery, or life cycle assessment, depends heavily on the **quality of the underlying data**. Inaccurate or unreliable data can compromise project design, lead to non-compliance with environmental regulations, or result in unsustainable decision-making. Therefore, **rigorous Quality Assurance (QA)** and **Quality Control (QC)** protocols must be integrated at every stage of data collection and analysis.

Key Principles of High-Quality Environmental Data

1. **Accuracy**

   Accuracy refers to the closeness of a measured value to the true or accepted reference value. In environmental sampling, accuracy is critical to ensure that the reported values reflect actual field or laboratory conditions. For example, measuring the lead content in soil must reflect the real concentration that exists in situ; otherwise, risk assessments and remediation strategies may be flawed.

Dr. Akshay Gupta, Dr. Chandra Prakash Gour, Dr. Anulipi Agrawal,
Er. Aaisha Sayyed

2. **Precision**

Precision indicates the degree of agreement among repeated measurements of the same sample under identical conditions. High precision demonstrates that the measurement process is reliable, even if the measurements are slightly biased. For instance, three readings of COD (Chemical Oxygen Demand) for the same water sample that yield values of 248, 251, and 249 mg/L illustrate good precision.

3. **Repeatability**

Repeatability reflects the ability to produce consistent results when the same method is applied under the same conditions, either over time or by different operators. This is essential in long-term monitoring programs or when comparing laboratory analyses across institutions.

Standard QA/QC Practices in Environmental Laboratories

To ensure data meets these criteria, environmental laboratories follow structured QA/QC protocols. These practices are mandated by accreditation bodies such as the National Environmental Laboratory Accreditation Conference (NELAC) in the United States and equivalent agencies worldwide.

Common QA/QC Measures Include:

- **Standard Operating Procedures (SOPs):** Every analytical method should be governed by a documented SOP that outlines detailed, step-by-step procedures for sample preparation, analysis, instrument calibration, data recording, and troubleshooting. SOPs ensure consistency across operators and over time.

- **Sampling Strategy and Planning:** A well-designed sampling plan helps achieve representativeness and accounts for spatial and temporal variability. The plan includes sampling locations, frequency, equipment used, preservation methods, and transportation logistics.

- **Chain-of-Custody Documentation:** This process ensures that sample integrity is maintained from collection through analysis. A chain-of-custody form tracks who handled the sample, at what time, and for what purpose—providing legal and scientific accountability.

- **Instrument Calibration and Maintenance:** Instruments must be regularly calibrated using standard solutions to ensure accurate readings. Calibration check standards, blanks, and quality control samples are run with each batch to validate instrument performance.

- **Data Validation and Verification:** Analytical results undergo internal verification by qualified personnel and are often subject to peer review or audit before being released. Anomalous data points are investigated, and if necessary, reanalysis is performed.

- **Internal Audits and Proficiency Testing:** Laboratories periodically audit their procedures and participate in inter-laboratory comparisons to ensure compliance with QA standards and identify areas for improvement.

Statistical Treatment of Data

Understanding Distribution Types in Environmental Analysis

In environmental engineering and sustainability science, the reliability of any analytical or modelling outcome hinges on the ability to accurately interpret and handle environmental data. A foundational step in this process is understanding the **type of distribution** that the data follows. The distribution type determines how we summarize, analyze, and draw conclusions from the data, and ultimately guides key decisions in design, compliance, and risk management.

Why Distribution Type Matters?

Statistical distribution describes how data points are spread or arranged across a range of values. In environmental studies, distribution type influences:

- The selection of appropriate measures of central tendency (mean, median, mode),

- The type of statistical tests applied (parametric vs. non-parametric),

- The accuracy of extrapolating sample data to population-level conclusions.

Incorrect assumptions about data distribution can lead to errors in interpretation, potentially affecting public health decisions, environmental impact assessments, and compliance with regulatory limits.

Common Distribution Types in Environmental Data

1. Log-Normal Distribution

Definition and Characteristics: A log-normal distribution occurs when the logarithms of the dataset values form a normal (bell-shaped) distribution. In this distribution:

- Most data points cluster near the lower end of the scale,

- A few large values skew the dataset, forming a long right-hand tail,

- The arithmetic mean is usually greater than the median and mode.

Its Occurrence in Environmental Data: Environmental data often spans several orders of magnitude and is influenced by numerous interacting variables (e.g., weather, human activity, soil properties). As a result, it's common to observe skewed datasets, especially when measuring pollutant concentrations in air, water, or soil.

Examples:

- Heavy metal concentrations in industrially impacted soils,

- Bacterial counts in river water,

- Airborne particulate matter in urban environments.

Statistical Approach: When dealing with log-normal data following things should be taken care of:

- Use geometric mean (rather than arithmetic mean) as a measure of central tendency,

- Apply log-transformation before performing statistical analysis (e.g., ANOVA, regression),

- Interpret results in the transformed and back-transformed scale for clarity.

2. Normal Distribution

Definition and Characteristics: A normal distribution, often called a Gaussian distribution, is symmetric and bell-shaped. It indicates that data points are evenly distributed around the mean:

- The mean, median, and mode are all equal,

- Approximately 68% of data falls within one standard deviation of the mean,

- The probability density function is symmetrical.

When It Occurs: Environmental data may follow a normal distribution when:

- The system is relatively homogeneous, with minimal variability,

- Data are averaged over space or time (e.g., daily average temperatures),

- The sample size is large, and random errors are evenly distributed.

Examples:

- pH measurements from treated wastewater effluent,

- Daily mean temperature records,

- Concentrations of stable parameters in groundwater with low anthropogenic impact.

Statistical Approach: For normally distributed data following things should be noted:

- Use arithmetic mean and standard deviation for summary statistics,

- Employ parametric tests like t-tests, ANOVA, and linear regression without transformation.

The distribution type and its brief description are given in Table 3.4.

Data Interpretation

Interpreting environmental data is a crucial step in transforming raw measurements into actionable insights. In sustainable engineering, these interpretations guide decisions in areas such as risk assessment, environmental compliance, infrastructure design, and life cycle analysis. To derive meaningful conclusions, engineers and scientists use various statistical tools that help describe the behavior, reliability, and trends within datasets.

This section provides a deeper look into three foundational concepts in environmental data interpretation: central tendency, data variability, and confidence estimation.

Table 3.4: Brief description of distribution types

Distribution Type	Central Tendency	Used for
Log-Normal	Geometric Mean	Pollutant concentrations, microbes
Normal	Arithmetic Mean	Temperature, pH, noise levels

1. Mean, Median, and Mode: Central Tendency Indicators

Central tendency measures describe where most values in a dataset cluster. Each measure offers a unique perspective:

- **Mean (Arithmetic Average):** The sum of all data values divided by the number of observations. It provides a general estimate of the central value and is useful when data are symmetrically distributed (i.e., normally distributed). However, the mean is sensitive to extreme values (outliers), which can distort its representativeness.

$$\text{Mean} = \frac{\sum x_i}{n}$$

- **Median:**

  The middle value when the data are arranged in ascending order. It is robust against outliers and is preferred in skewed or non-normally distributed datasets (e.g., log-normal). The median better represents the "typical" value in such cases.

- **Mode:**

  The value that appears most frequently in the dataset. It is especially useful for categorical or discrete data (e.g., most common pollutant level category) and in identifying recurring environmental conditions.

2. Variance and Standard Deviation: Measures of Data Spread

While central tendency provides a focal point, it is equally important to understand how much the data varies around that point.

- **Variance (σ^2):** Measures the average of the squared deviations from the mean. It quantifies how spread out the data points are. A higher variance indicates greater dispersion in the dataset.

$$\text{Variance} = \frac{\sum(x_i - \bar{x})^2}{n}$$

- **Standard Deviation (σ):** The square root of the variance, representing data spread in the same units as the data. It gives a clearer sense of variability in practical terms. In normally distributed data, approximately 68% of the values lie within one standard deviation of the mean, and 95% within two.

$$\text{Standard Deviation} = \sqrt{\text{Variance}}$$

3. Upper Confidence Limit (UCL): A Conservative Estimate for Decision-Making

In regulatory and risk assessment contexts, uncertainty is inherent due to sampling limitations and natural variability. To account for this, environmental engineers use confidence intervals, particularly the Upper Confidence Limit (UCL) of the mean.

Dr. Akshay Gupta, Dr. Chandra Prakash Gour, Dr. Anulipi Agrawal, Er. Aaisha Sayyed

UCL represents a statistically derived boundary above which the true population mean is unlikely to lie, based on the observed sample. It provides a conservative estimate that helps ensure protective decision-making under uncertainty.

$$\text{UCL} = \bar{x} + t \cdot \left(\frac{s}{\sqrt{n}} \right)$$

Where:

$\bar{x}$ = sample mean

t = t-value from the Student's t-distribution at desired confidence level (e.g., 95%)

s = sample standard deviation

n = sample size

Numerical Examples

Example 1: *You analyzed 6 samples of recycled paper for cadmium (Cd) content. The concentrations (µg/g) were: 0.32, 0.35, 0.30, 0.33, 0.31, 0.34*

Calculate the 95% Upper Confidence Limit (UCL) for the average concentration. (Use t value as 2.571)

Solution:

Step 1: Calculate the Mean (x̄)

$$\bar{x} = \frac{0.32 + 0.35 + 0.30 + 0.33 + 0.31 + 0.34}{6} = \frac{1.95}{6} = 0.325 \, \mu g/g$$

Step 2: Calculate the Standard Deviation (s)

$$s \approx 0.0187 \, \mu g/g$$

Step 3: Degrees of freedom = n - 1 = 5

$$t_{(0.05,5)} = 2.571 \, (\text{from t-table})$$

Step 4: Standard Error (SE):

$$SE = \frac{s}{\sqrt{n}} = \frac{0.0187}{\sqrt{6}} \approx 0.00764$$

Step 5: Calculate UCL:

$$UCL = \bar{x} + t \cdot SE = 0.325 + 2.571 \cdot 0.00764 \approx 0.325 + 0.0196 = 0.3446$$

Unsolved Example 2: *You tested 10 samples of recycled cover paper for lead (Pb). The results in µg/g are: 0.85, 0.89, 0.87, 0.86, 0.88, 0.90, 0.84, 0.91, 0.89, 0.88*

Calculate the 95% UCL. (Obtain the value of t from the t-Table)

Case Example: TCLP Analysis for Lead

Proper classification of waste is a foundational task in sustainable waste management. Misclassification, either overestimating or underestimating the hazard posed, can lead to severe environmental consequences or unnecessary expenditure. The Toxicity Characteristic Leaching Procedure (TCLP), developed by the U.S. Environmental Protection Agency (EPA), is one of the most widely used methods for determining whether a solid waste exhibits hazardous characteristics.

This test simulates the leaching process a waste would undergo in a sanitary landfill, where it may come into contact with acidic liquids. It is particularly useful for predicting the potential for contaminants such as heavy metals to migrate into groundwater.

Dr. Akshay Gupta, Dr. Chandra Prakash Gour, Dr. Anulipi Agrawal,
Er. Aaisha Sayyed

Purpose of TCLP

The TCLP is designed to determine whether a waste material releases harmful substances—such as lead, cadmium, arsenic, or mercury—in concentrations that exceed regulatory thresholds. If a contaminant exceeds its respective limit in the TCLP leachate, the waste is considered hazardous under the Resource Conservation and Recovery Act (RCRA) and must be managed accordingly.

- For lead, the regulatory TCLP limit is 5 mg/L. Exceeding this value indicates the waste has the potential to leach harmful levels of lead under landfill conditions, posing risks to groundwater quality and public health.

Case Study: TCLP Testing of Electronic Waste

Electronic waste (e-waste), such as discarded circuit boards, batteries, and cathode ray tubes, often contains significant concentrations of lead. Proper disposal of e-waste is essential to prevent long-term contamination of soil and water systems. This case example analyzes two datasets derived from TCLP testing of e-waste samples, illustrating the use of statistical techniques to interpret results and guide waste management decisions.

Dataset 1: Normally Distributed Results

- **Number of Samples (n):** 29

- **Mean Concentration:** 4.83 mg/L

- **Standard Deviation:** 2.0 mg/L

In this case, the data followed a normal (bell-shaped) distribution, which is relatively uncommon in environmental sampling but may occur when the waste material is homogenous or well-mixed. The arithmetic mean of 4.83 mg/L is below the regulatory limit of 5 mg/L.

Given the moderate standard deviation and normal distribution, this dataset suggests that most samples are within an acceptable range. Since the mean and variability are within limits, and assuming confidence intervals and UCL (Upper Confidence Limit) checks confirm compliance, this waste may be considered non-hazardous and suitable for disposal in a municipal solid waste landfill.

Dataset 2: Log-Normally Distributed Results

- **Number of Samples (n):** 31

- **Geometric Mean (after log transformation):** 4.28 mg/L

- **Distribution Type:** Log-normal

Dr. Akshay Gupta, Dr. Chandra Prakash Gour, Dr. Anulipi Agrawal,
Er. Aaisha Sayyed

The second dataset exhibited a log-normal distribution, which is more typical of environmental data. This indicates that most data points are clustered near the lower end, with a few significantly higher values pulling the arithmetic mean upwards.

Since log-normal distributions are skewed, geometric mean is a more appropriate measure of central tendency. At 4.28 mg/L, the geometric mean is below the regulatory threshold. However, due to the presence of higher values in the dataset, a UCL calculation is essential to assess compliance conservatively.

Upon applying the UCL method (e.g., 95% confidence level), if the UCL remains below 5 mg/L, the dataset can be interpreted as compliant. This additional statistical check ensures that, even accounting for variability and sampling uncertainty, the waste does not pose an unacceptable risk.

Conclusion

In the pursuit of sustainable development, data is more than just numbers, it is the evidence based upon which responsible engineering decisions are built. Environmental data collection and interpretation serve as the cornerstone of sustainable engineering, informing every phase of a project from planning and design to implementation, monitoring, and eventual decommissioning or restoration.

This chapter has taken a comprehensive look at the entire life cycle of environmental data, beginning with the collection of samples—whether from air, water, soil, or waste, and progressing through the critical stages of physical and chemical preparation. The various analytical instruments and procedures described, ranging from titrations to sophisticated spectrometric and chromatographic techniques, highlight the diversity of tools available to environmental engineers. These techniques, when properly selected and applied, generate the precise and meaningful data required for environmental assessment.

A particular emphasis was placed on quality assurance (QA) and quality control (QC), both of which are non-negotiable components of any credible data collection and analysis process. By implementing rigorous QA/QC protocols, such as calibration curves, blanks, spiked samples, replicates, and proper chain-of-custody documentation, engineers ensure the integrity, accuracy, and reproducibility of environmental data.

Furthermore, the chapter explored the statistical treatment of environmental data, recognizing the inherent variability and complexity of natural systems. By distinguishing between normal and log-normal distributions, understanding central tendencies and variability, and applying tools like the Upper Confidence Limit (UCL), engineers can derive sound, defensible conclusions, even in the presence of uncertainty.

Dr. Akshay Gupta, Dr. Chandra Prakash Gour, Dr. Anulipi Agrawal,
Er. Aaisha Sayyed

The practical relevance of these concepts was underscored through a case study involving TCLP analysis for lead in electronic waste, illustrating how statistical interpretation directly influences regulatory classification, risk assessment, and waste management decisions.

Finally, all these elements converge in the Life Cycle Assessment (LCA) framework. LCA relies heavily on accurate and representative environmental data to quantify the environmental impacts of products, processes, and systems. The quality of an LCA is only as strong as the data it is built upon, making data collection and analysis not just a technical formality, but a moral and environmental imperative in the quest for sustainability.

In essence, robust environmental data is the bedrock of sustainable engineering. By embracing a disciplined approach to sampling, analysis, validation, and interpretation, engineers and researchers can uphold the highest standards of scientific integrity, contribute meaningfully to policy and regulation, and lead the way in building a more resilient, resource-efficient, and environmentally conscious future.

Exercises

Q. 1: Explain the significance of environmental data collection in sustainable engineering.

Q. 2: Describe the steps involved in physical and chemical sample preparation.

Q. 3: Compare the roles of the three key analytical instruments commonly used in environmental laboratories.

Q. 4: Elaborate on the concept of QA/QC in environmental data analysis.

Q. 5: Differentiate between normal and log-normal data distributions.

Q. 6: Define and explain the concept of the Upper Confidence Limit (UCL).

Q. 7: A TCLP test for lead on an e-waste sample yields the following results:

- *Dataset A: Normally distributed with a mean of 4.83 mg/L and a standard deviation of 2.0 mg/L*

- *Dataset B: Log-normally distributed with a geometric mean of 4.28 mg/L and a calculated 95% UCL of 4.92 mg/L*

Assuming the regulatory threshold for lead is 5.0 mg/L, analyze whether the samples are compliant. Justify your conclusion based on statistical interpretation and regulatory considerations.

Dr. Akshay Gupta, Dr. Chandra Prakash Gour, Dr. Anulipi Agrawal,
Er. Aaisha Sayyed

Q. 8: Discuss the role of representative sampling in environmental data collection.

4. Green and Sustainable Materials

Introduction: Why Materials Matter

Every product we create begins with a material. From the infrastructure that sustains our cities to the devices we rely on day to day, materials are the foundation of modern life. However, our growing consumption is placing unprecedented pressure on the planet's finite resources. We extract, process, manufacture, and discard with little regard for the long-term implications. The resulting impacts—deforestation, pollution, greenhouse gas emissions, and social inequities—are now impossible to ignore.

Sustainability in materials is not a luxury or trend; it is a necessity. This chapter explores the idea of green and sustainable materials, not just as a technical solution but as a philosophical shift in how we relate to the material world. Through science, design, policy, and ethics, we aim to uncover how materials can be harnessed to support a prosperous yet sustainable future.

Defining Sustainability for Materials

Sustainability is often described as meeting the needs of the present without compromising the ability of future generations to meet their own needs. For materials, this involves managing extraction, use, and disposal in a way that preserves ecosystems, supports human well-being, and sustains economic systems.

Resource Acquisition

The life of a material starts with extraction from the Earth. This could be mining metals from ore, tapping rubber trees, or harvesting timber. The process of resource acquisition is fraught with environmental and social challenges. Mining can lead to habitat destruction, water pollution, toxic tailings, and significant carbon emissions. Deforestation reduces biodiversity, contributes to climate change, and disrupts the lives of Indigenous communities.

Sustainable resource acquisition is prioritized differently. The different priorities of sustainable resource acquisition are given below:

- Using renewable resources at a rate that does not exceed regeneration.
- Employing low-impact mining techniques.
- Enforcing fair labour practices and community consent.

- Utilizing secondary sources through urban mining and recycling.

Processing and Use

Processing materials into usable products, whether that involves smelting aluminum, manufacturing steel, or refining crude oil into plastic, is typically an energy-intensive process. It also creates pollution, from carbon emissions to chemical effluents.

A sustainable approach to material processing involves the following processes:

- Energy efficiency in industrial processes.

- Clean and renewable energy sources.

- Minimization of waste and byproducts.

- Lifecycle thinking in product design.

Material use, too, must be examined. The way we design products—how long they last, how easily they can be repaired or recycled—has a profound impact on sustainability.

End-of-Life

Every product eventually reaches the end of its useful life. It may be thrown away, recycled, repurposed, or allowed to degrade. Sustainable materials are those that:

- Can be easily and safely recycled.

- Biodegrade into non-toxic components.

- Retain value in secondary markets.

Poor end-of-life outcomes are a major driver of environmental degradation. E-waste, for instance, often ends up in developing countries where it is dismantled in unsafe conditions. Sustainable systems must be designed to support safe, equitable, and efficient material recovery.

Measuring Environmental Impact: The Life Cycle Assessment (LCA)

Life Cycle Assessment (LCA) is a scientific method used to evaluate the environmental impacts associated with all stages of a product's life. An LCA considers:

- Raw material extraction.

- Material processing.

- Manufacturing.

- Distribution and retail.

- Use phase.

- End-of-life treatment and disposal.

Dr. Akshay Gupta, Dr. Chandra Prakash Gour, Dr. Anulipi Agrawal,
Er. Aaisha Sayyed

By examining the full cradle-to-grave journey of a material, LCA helps avoid the common pitfall of shifting burdens from one life stage to another. For example, while electric vehicles produce fewer tailpipe emissions than gasoline cars, their batteries require the mining of lithium and cobalt. An LCA provides a holistic picture to guide better decision-making. The complete lifecycle analysis through pictorial representation is shown in Figure 4.1.

LCA results are often expressed in terms of environmental impact categories such as:

- Global warming potential (carbon footprint).

- Acidification potential.

- Eutrophication potential.

- Human toxicity.

- Resource depletion.

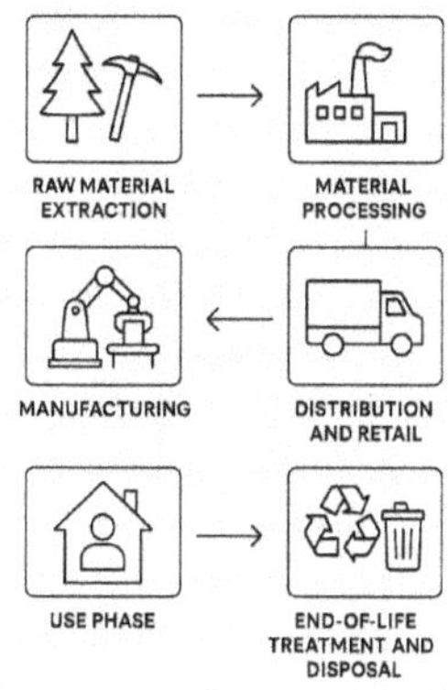

Figure 4.1: Life Cycle of a Product

Material Abundance and Scarcity

Materials vary in abundance across the Earth's crust. This has direct implications for sustainability, economics, and geopolitical stability.

Abundant Materials

Materials like oxygen, silicon, aluminum, and iron are abundant. These elements form the basis of glass, concrete, and metal alloys used widely in construction and infrastructure. Their abundance allows for economies of scale and relative sustainability, though processing can still be energy-intensive.

Scarce and Critical Materials

In contrast, materials like tantalum, neodymium, dysprosium, and platinum are rare and difficult to extract. These critical materials are vital to high-tech applications, including smartphones, wind turbines, and electric vehicles. However, their scarcity poses challenges:

- Increased environmental impact per unit.

- Greater price volatility.

- Dependency on specific geographic regions (e.g., China for rare earths).

•	Potential for supply chain disruption.

To mitigate these issues, we must:

•	Develop substitution materials

•	Improve recycling and recovery

The Sherwood Relationship and Resource Economics

The Sherwood Plot, developed by Thomas Sherwood, illustrates a key principle: the cost of purifying a material increases exponentially as its concentration in the source material decreases.

For example:

•	High-concentration ores (like bauxite for aluminum) are economical to extract.

•	Low-concentration ores or dispersed sources (like gold in seawater) are prohibitively expensive.

This principle highlights why recycling is often more cost-effective and sustainable than mining virgin materials. If a metal can be recovered from urban waste or obsolete electronics, the energy and cost savings are significant.

This relationship also stresses the importance of:

- Avoiding excessive dilution in waste streams.

- Designing products for easy material separation.

- Prioritizing recycling over downcycling.

Reserve Lifespans: How Long Can We Sustain Use?

Geologists estimate the lifespan of known material reserves based on current usage patterns and available technology. However, these figures can be misleading.

They assume the following for the estimation of the lifespan:

- Constant rates of consumption.

- No discoveries or technological breakthroughs.

- No improvements in recycling.

Even with these assumptions, the data is sobering:

- Silver: Less than 20 years of supply at current rates.

- Copper: 100 years, but increasing demand for electrification could shorten this.

- Antimony and Tin: Facing depletion in under two decades.

Dr. Akshay Gupta, Dr. Chandra Prakash Gour, Dr. Anulipi Agrawal,
Er. Aaisha Sayyed

To ensure material longevity, following measures should be taken:

- Improve recycling infrastructure.

- Promote product longevity and repair.

- Reduce per-capita material consumption.

Tracking Material Flows

Material Flow Analysis (MFA) is a technique used to map the movement of materials through economies. It helps quantify inputs, stocks, and outputs across sectors and is vital for designing sustainable systems.

Example: Lead in the U.S.

In 1970, the majority of lead in the U.S. was used in gasoline additives and paint. These applications released lead into the environment, creating public health crises.

By the 1990s, regulatory changes phased out leaded gasoline. Lead use shifted toward battery products with high recovery rates. Recycling rates increased from 3% to over 65%, significantly reducing lead emissions and health risks.

MFA helps in the following:

- Identify bottlenecks in recycling.

- Guide policy on import/export regulations.

- Prioritize materials for investment and innovation.

Recycling: The Cornerstone of Material Sustainability

Recycling is one of the most effective strategies for achieving material sustainability. It reduces the need for virgin extraction, lowers energy use, and minimizes waste.

Yet not all materials are recycled equally:

- Aluminum: High recycling rate due to economic viability and low processing energy.
- Glass: Often downcycled due to impurities.
- Plastics: Fragmented systems and polymer complexity hinder recycling.
- Rare Earths: Technical barriers and lack of infrastructure.

Improving recycling requires the following:

- Standardized product labelling.

- Robust collection systems.

- Investment in separation and sorting technologies.

Dr. Akshay Gupta, Dr. Chandra Prakash Gour, Dr. Anulipi Agrawal,
Er. Aaisha Sayyed

-     Consumer education.

Industrial Ecology and Circular Economy

Industrial ecology treats industrial systems as analogues to natural ecosystems, where outputs from one process become inputs for another. The circular economy builds on this idea, promoting closed-loop systems where waste is minimized and materials retain value.

Key principles include:

- Designing for durability, repair, and recyclability.
- Maintaining and sharing products (e.g., leasing models).
- Cascading use (reusing materials for multiple purposes before recycling).

Governments and corporations are beginning to integrate circular strategies into policy and business models. The European Union's Circular Economy Action Plan and companies like Interface and Patagonia exemplify these shifts.

Designing for Sustainability

Sustainable design goes beyond choosing greener materials. It is about integrating sustainability into every phase of product development:

- Material selection: Favor low-impact, recycled, or bio-based materials
- Design for disassembly: Allow parts to be easily separated and replaced
- Modularity: Enable upgrades without replacing entire systems
- Standardization: Use compatible components to simplify recycling
- Minimalism: Reduce material use without compromising function

Eco-design thinking must be taught and institutionalized across industries to create a scalable impact.

The Role of Policy and Innovation

Regulations and incentives can accelerate sustainable material use:

- Extended Producer Responsibility (EPR): Holds manufacturers accountable for end-of-life disposal.
- Eco-labelling: Informs consumers of environmental impact.
- Tax credits: Encourage R&D in recycling technologies and green materials.

Innovation also plays a crucial role:

- AI and machine learning: Improve sorting and material recovery.

- Green chemistry: Reduces toxicity and improves recyclability.

- Blockchain: Enables material traceability in supply chains.

Case Study: Aluminium

Aluminium showcases the potential of circular material systems:

- Abundant in nature, but energy-intensive to produce.

- Exceptionally lightweight and strong.

- Recyclable without loss of quality.

Recycled aluminium requires 95% less energy and generates only 5% of the greenhouse gas emissions of primary production. The metal is used in transportation, packaging, construction, and more often with closed-loop recycling systems in place.

Challenges remain in:

- Contaminant removal.

- Mixed alloy separation.

- Collection logistics.

Case Study: Rare Earth Elements in Electronics

Rare earth elements (REEs) are critical to modern technologies:

- Used in hard drives, electric motors, wind turbines, etc.
- Extraction is complex and environmentally damaging.
- Recycling is technologically challenging due to small quantities and complex assemblies.

Strategies to improve REE sustainability include:

- Product design that facilitates recovery.

- Mechanical and chemical separation technologies.

- Government-supported recovery programs.

Future Directions: Biomaterials and Urban Mining

Biomaterials

Biomaterials are derived from renewable sources and are often biodegradable:

- Mycelium: Fungal networks used to grow packaging and insulation.
- Algae plastics: Biodegradable alternatives to petroleum-based polymers.
- Bamboo composites: Strong, fast-growing alternative to timber and plastics.

These materials offer reduced environmental impact, but challenges remain in scalability, performance, and infrastructure compatibility.

Urban Mining

Urban mining involves extracting valuable materials from electronic waste, old buildings, and landfills. Cities become new "mines" for copper, gold, and rare earths.

Key benefits:

- Reduces the need for destructive mining.

- Capitalizes on high material concentration in e-waste.

- Creates local economic opportunities.

Conclusion: The Ethics of Material Choice

Sustainable material use is far more than a matter of engineering efficiency or economic feasibility. It is a profound ethical responsibility of a human being to use sustainable material and follow the sustainable practices. Each choice we make in selecting materials, designing products, and shaping supply chains carries long-lasting consequences. These decisions affect not only our immediate surroundings but also the lives of future generations and the ecological systems that sustain all life.

The materials we extract and use today come with a footprint that stretches across time and space. From the deforestation caused by paper production, to the carbon emissions of cement manufacturing, to the e-waste generated by electronics, the impacts are cumulative and often invisible. Thus, every material decision becomes a statement of our values. Are we prioritizing convenience and cost, or are we valuing sustainability, justice, and resilience?

Embracing life cycle thinking helps illuminate these hidden impacts. It pushes us to look beyond the product's surface and consider its entire journey, from raw material extraction, processing, and use, to disposal or reuse. With this mindset, sustainability becomes embedded in every stage of design and production.

Furthermore, innovation plays a crucial role in advancing this ethical transformation. New materials, bio-based polymers, recycled composites, and carbon-neutral alternatives are rapidly emerging to replace outdated, environmentally harmful ones. Technological advancements must be harnessed to create smarter, lighter, and more regenerative materials that not only meet performance demands but also reduce harm to the planet.

But even innovation is not enough without equity and ecological integrity. A sustainable future must be inclusive, ensuring that communities on the frontlines of resource extraction, waste disposal, and climate change are heard, respected, and empowered. The shift toward sustainable materials must uplift all, not just the few.

Ultimately, the materials of the future will be judged not just by their strength, cost, or beauty, but by the values they represent. They will shape the walls of our homes, the frames of our vehicles, the circuits of our technology, but more importantly, they will shape the ethical and ecological foundations of our civilization.

By making responsible material choices today, we do not just build better products, we build a more just, resilient, and sustainable world.

Exercises

Q. 1: What are sustainable materials?

Q. 2: Differentiate between abundant and critical materials.

Q. 3: List the main stages of Life Cycle Assessment (LCA).

Q. 4: Why is recycling important for sustainability?

Q. 5: What does the Sherwood Plot explain?

Q. 6: State key principles of the circular economy.

Q. 7: How is aluminum an example of a closed-loop system?

Q. 8: How would you design a more sustainable smartphone?

5. Case Studies

Introduction

In the discourse of sustainability, measurement is essential. Without quantifiable data, environmental claims remain speculative. Life Cycle Assessment (LCA) provides a rigorous framework to evaluate the environmental impacts of products, services, and systems throughout their entire life span, from raw material extraction to end-of-life disposal. In this chapter, we explore LCA not just as a methodology but as a decision-making tool that enables sustainable design, policy formation, and technological innovation.

Framework of LCA

Life Cycle Assessment is fundamentally a four-stage process. The detailed framework of LCA through a flowchart is shown in Figure 5.1.

1. **Goal and Scope Definition**: Establishes the purpose of the LCA and defines the functional unit for the basis for comparing systems (e.g., "drying one pair of hands" or "providing 500 ml of potable water").

2. **Life Cycle Inventory (LCI)**: Involves collecting data on material inputs, energy use, emissions, and waste across the life cycle of the product or process.

3. **Life Cycle Impact Assessment (LCIA)**: Translates inventory data into potential environmental impacts using indicators such as global warming potential, acidification, or human toxicity.

4. **Interpretation**: Involves analyzing the results to inform decisions, identify improvement areas, or support policy and marketing claims.

The IPAT Equation: Quantifying Environmental Impact

An insightful way to understand the drivers of environmental degradation is through the IPAT equation:

$$I = P \times A \times T$$

Where:

- I is the total environmental impact,

- P is the population,

- A is affluence (GDP per capita),

- T is the technology factor (impact per unit of GDP).

In a practical application, projecting the impact from 2010 to 2060 using modest annual growth rates (e.g., 1% population growth, 2% affluence, and 1% improvement in technology efficiency) results in a 7.28% increase in environmental impact. However, under higher growth assumptions (2%, 3%, and 2%, respectively), the impact balloons to 31.76%, highlighting how minor variations in growth assumptions can dramatically alter long-term outcomes.

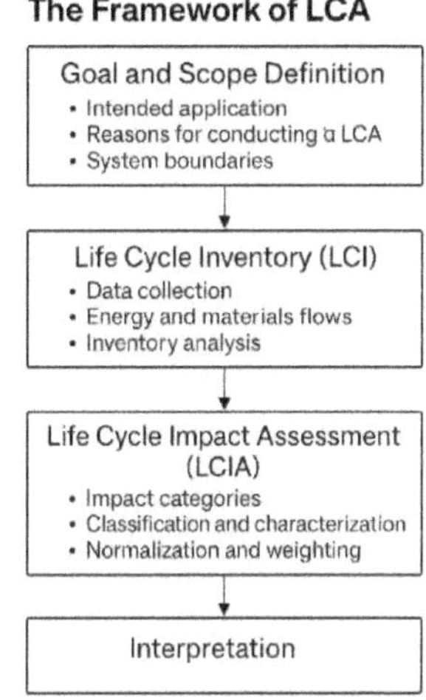

Figure 5.1: Flowchart for the Framework of LCA

LCA in Practice: Case Studies

Case Study 1: Paper Towel vs. Hand Dryer

A comparative LCA conducted in a Canadian university evaluated the environmental impacts of hand drying systems: electric hand dryers versus paper towels. Using "drying a pair of hands" as the functional unit, both systems were analyzed from cradle to grave.

- **Hand Dryers**: High energy consumption, heavily dependent on the electricity source. Better in scenarios with renewable energy grids.

- **Paper Towels**: If made from recycled paper and composted post-use, they often outperformed hand dryers in global warming potential and human toxicity impacts.

Key insight: **Context matters.** A paper towel might be more sustainable in one region and less so in another, depending on waste infrastructure and electricity mix.

Case Study 2: Bioplastics vs. PET Bottles

Another study compared polylactic acid (PLA) — a bioplastic — with conventional polyethylene terephthalate (PET) bottles. The functional unit was the production of 1000 bottles (500 ml each).

While PLA, derived from corn starch, appeared environmentally friendlier in fossil fuel use, its impacts on freshwater eutrophication and land use were higher due to agricultural cultivation. Moreover, most waste scenarios (e.g., landfill or incineration) posed challenges, particularly for bioplastics that require specific industrial composting conditions.

Dr. Akshay Gupta, Dr. Chandra Prakash Gour, Dr. Anulipi Agrawal,
Er. Aaisha Sayyed

The conclusion? PLA isn't a universal fix. End-of-life treatment and agricultural inputs must be considered when assessing bio-based alternatives.

Energy and Emissions: A Bulb's Story

The humble light bulb also offers insights. Consider the extra electricity used when a 25W incandescent bulb replaces a 5W fluorescent bulb over 1000 hours: a 20-kWh increase. But considering 15% transmission losses and 40% power plant efficiency, the actual energy input becomes 58.82 kWh. To produce this from coal (8 kWh/kg heat content), 7.35 kg of coal is required.

These seemingly simple choices — one bulb over another — cascade into significant energy and material consequences, illustrating the potency of LCA at a consumer behavior level.

Risk and Exposure in Environmental Analysis

LCA isn't limited to products. It can also model **exposure and risk**. Consider a problem where 10,000 people die annually from vehicular accidents in a state of 100 million people. This yields a per capita risk. By applying this rate to a city with 5 million people over 2 days, the expected fatalities can be computed using:

$$\text{Risk} = \text{Population} \times \text{Exposure Time} \times \text{Hazard Rate}$$

The result, approximately 2.74 deaths, demonstrates how risk modeling can quantify micro-level outcomes using macro data.

Mass Balance and Control Volumes

In environmental engineering, the mass balance approach helps model pollutant flow and transformations. A control volume (e.g., a lake) receives inflow from a river and has internal sources (e.g., microbial reactions) and sinks (e.g., outflow, sedimentation). The governing equation is:

Change in Storage = Input − Output + Sources − Sinks

At steady state, storage change is zero, simplifying the analysis. For example, if a chemical manufacturing plant discharges a contaminant into a lake, LCA can model how much of the pollutant remains based on inflow, degradation rates, and volume.

Odour: An Existing Problem

Odours typically come from a blend of many compounds, interacting in complex ways, which makes detection and treatment difficult. There may be various odour sources that make it difficult to detect the actual odour source.

Dr. Akshay Gupta, Dr. Chandra Prakash Gour, Dr. Anulipi Agrawal, Er. Aaisha Sayyed

Common Odour Sources:

Hydrogen sulphide (H_2S) – "Rotten egg" smell; common in sewage and anaerobic decay.

Organic sulphur compounds – Strong, persistent odours from industrial processes.

Organic sulphides – Found in decaying organic matter.

Ammonia – Pungent smell; from animal waste, fertilizer production.

Amines – Fishy odours; found in decomposition and chemical industries.

Fatty Acids – Rancid or sour odours; common in food waste.

Aromatics – Sweet or pungent smells; includes compounds like benzene or toluene.

Methyl-ethyl ketone (MEK) – Solvent-like smell; used in coatings and plastics.

Terpenes – Pine or citrus-like smells; natural VOCs from plants, but can become problematic in high concentrations.

Odour Control in Composting Facilities

In another LCA, researchers assessed odour control technologies at composting sites. There are seven different ways developed for the removal of existing odours. The basic odour control technologies that are used for odour control are shown in Figure 5.2.

Biofilters

Use microorganisms to biologically degrade odorous compounds in a moist, organic medium (like compost or peat).

Effective for treating air with low concentrations of biodegradable odours.

Activated Carbon Adsorption

Odorous molecules adhere to the surface of activated carbon.

Works best for removing volatile organic compounds (VOCs) and sulphur-based odours.

Packed-bed Wet Scrubbers

Gas streams pass through a packed column where a scrubbing liquid absorbs contaminants.

Suitable for soluble or chemically reactive odours.

Fine Mist Wet Scrubbers

Similar to packed-bed, but uses fine mist for better contact and removal efficiency.

Dr. Akshay Gupta, Dr. Chandra Prakash Gour, Dr. Anulipi Agrawal,
Er. Aaisha Sayyed

Often used as pre-treatment or for particulate-bound odours.

Thermal Oxidization

Burns odorous compounds at high temperatures, converting them to less harmful substances like CO_2 and H_2O.

Highly effective, but energy-intensive.

Oxidization Chemicals

Chemicals like ozone or chlorine dioxide oxidize odorous compounds.

Can be used in gas or liquid phase; fast acting but must be handled carefully due to chemical hazards.

Masking Agents

Do not remove odours but cover them with stronger, more pleasant scents.

Used in situations where odour elimination is impractical or for temporary relief.

Interpretation and Limitations

LCA is not without limitations. Many datasets rely on average or modeled data. Impact categories might not capture localized effects (e.g., social equity, biodiversity). Yet, LCA remains a vital decision tool when used with transparency and appropriate context.

Key recommendations for effective LCA:

- Always define a clear functional unit and system boundary.

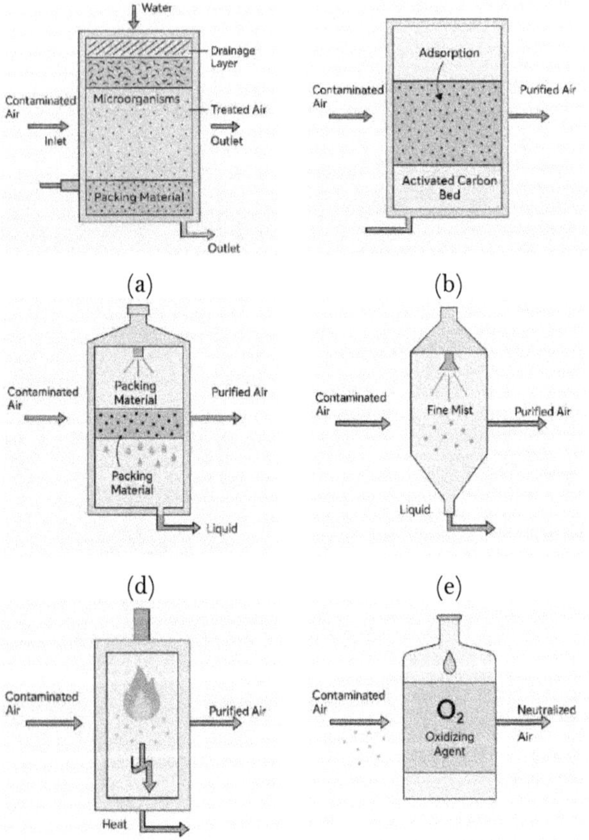

Figure 5.2: Methods for Odour Removal (a) Biofilter (b) Activated Carbon (c) Packed Bed Wet Scrubber (d) Fine Mist Wet Scrubber (e) Thermal Oxidization (f) Oxidization Chemicals

Dr. Akshay Gupta, Dr. Chandra Prakash Gour, Dr. Anulipi Agrawal,
Er. Aaisha Sayyed

- Choose relevant impact categories based on the product's life cycle.

- Use primary data where possible; otherwise, clearly state assumptions and uncertainties.

  Apply sensitivity analysis to test robustness.

The Bigger Picture: Policy and Design

Life Cycle Assessment (LCA) serves as a crucial link between environmental science and real-world decision-making, translating complex environmental data into actionable insights. It plays a pivotal role across various sectors by helping stakeholders understand the full environmental impact of a product, service, or process, from raw material extraction to end-of-life disposal.

For product designers, LCA provides a roadmap to identify and minimize environmental "hotspots". Hotspots are considered as the stages in the product life cycle that contribute disproportionately to environmental degradation. This enables more sustainable design choices, such as selecting eco-friendly materials, optimizing energy use, and improving recyclability.

For policymakers, LCA offers a data-driven foundation for shaping regulations and sustainability standards. One prominent example is Extended Producer Responsibility

(EPR), a policy approach that holds manufacturers accountable for the entire lifecycle of their products, especially their disposal. By integrating LCA insights, such policies become more targeted and effective, encouraging producers to adopt greener practices from the outset.

For consumers, LCA supports transparency by enabling more informed purchasing decisions. Environmental labels and declarations, often based on LCA data, allow individuals to consider the ecological footprint of products and services, empowering them to support sustainable practices through their consumption choices.

However, the true power of LCA emerges when it is integrated into a broader sustainability framework. This includes combining LCA with tools like Social Life Cycle Assessment (S-LCA), which evaluates social and socio-economic impacts across the life cycle; Cost-Benefit Analysis, which assesses economic trade-offs; and ethical considerations, which account for values such as intergenerational equity and environmental justice. When LCA is used alongside these metrics, it transforms from a technical tool into a holistic approach for sustainable development, guiding innovation, policy, and behavior toward long-term ecological and societal well-being. The flowchart diagram of policy and design is shown in Figure 5.3.

Dr. Akshay Gupta, Dr. Chandra Prakash Gour, Dr. Anulipi Agrawal, Er. Aaisha Sayyed

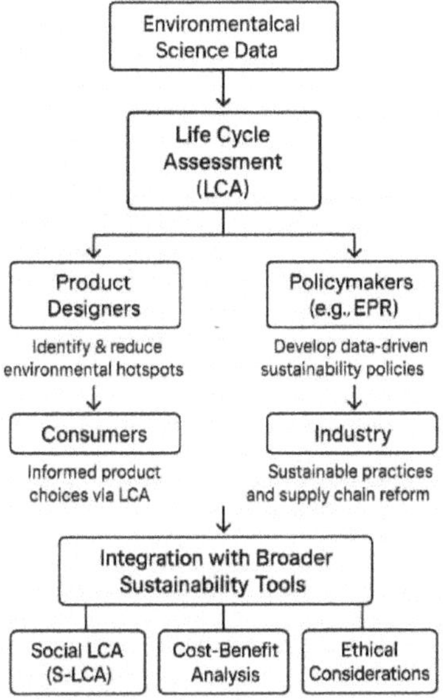

Figure 5.3: Policy and Design for the Life Cycle Assessment

Conclusion

Life Cycle Assessment (LCA) is not a perfect tool. No single method can capture the full complexity of our environmental challenges. Yet, in the pursuit of sustainability, LCA stands out as one of the most powerful instruments we have. It does not offer easy answers, but it brings clarity to complexity. By systematically evaluating the environmental impacts of a product or process from cradle to grave, LCA enables us to make informed, balanced decisions in a world full of trade-offs.

Whether we are choosing between paper towels and electric hand dryers, assessing the benefits of coal power versus solar panels, or comparing composting methods against landfill or incineration, LCA reveals the hidden costs and consequences that often go unnoticed. It pushes us to look beyond surface-level "green" claims and base our actions on evidence rather than assumptions. In doing so, it shifts the conversation from convenience and cost alone to one grounded in responsibility, systems thinking, and long-term impact.

As global pressures intensify, climate change, resource depletion, and pollution, our ability to measure, model, and mitigate environmental impacts becomes more than a technical exercise; it becomes a moral imperative. We can no longer afford to ignore the consequences of the materials we use, the energy we consume, or the waste we generate.

Incorporating LCA into design, policy, and industry allows us to anticipate trade-offs and minimize unintended harm. It enables innovation that is not only efficient but ethical. Ultimately, LCA empowers us to build a future where environmental stewardship is embedded into every product, every process, and every decision.

As we move forward, life cycle thinking will be an essential compass, guiding us not just toward better products but toward a more just, resilient, and sustainable world.

Dr. Akshay Gupta, Dr. Chandra Prakash Gour, Dr. Anulipi Agrawal,
Er. Aaisha Sayyed

Exercises

Q. 1: What are the four stages of LCA?

Q. 2: Use IPAT to estimate % impact increase for given growth rates.

Q. 3: Compare the LCA of paper towels vs. hand dryers.

Q. 4: What factors challenge the sustainability of PLA bottles?

Q. 5: Estimate city road deaths from state data (risk modelling).

Q. 6: Calculate the coal needed for a 100W bulb over 500 hours.

Q. 7: Explain all methods of odour control in detail.

Q. 8: Discuss the policy and design for the sustainable environmental procedures.

Authors Profile

Dr. Akshay Gupta

Dr. Akshay Gupta is an Assistant Professor at GH Raisoni College of Engineering and Management, Jalgaon. He holds a Ph.D. from the Indian Institute of Technology (IIT) Patna and an M.Tech in Structural Engineering from the National Institute of Technology (NIT) Silchar. His academic interests lie in advanced structural analysis and sustainable infrastructure development.

Dr. Chandra Prakash Gour

Dr. Chandra Prakash Gour serves as an Assistant Professor at GH Raisoni College of Engineering and Management, Jalgaon. He earned his Ph.D. from Maulana Azad National Institute of Technology (MANIT), Bhopal, and completed his M.Tech in Structural Engineering from UIT RGPV, Bhopal. His research areas include green concrete, structural optimization, and innovative construction materials.

Dr. Anulipi Agrawal

Dr. Anulipi Agrawal is a Counselor and Psychologist at GH Raisoni Public School, Jalgaon. She holds a Ph.D. in Psychology from Banasthali Vidyapith, Rajasthan. With a strong background in educational and developmental psychology, she is dedicated to supporting student well-being and mental health awareness.

Er. Aaisha Sayyed

Er. Aaisha Sayyed is an Assistant Professor at GH Raisoni College of Engineering and Management, Jalgaon. She is actively involved in teaching and mentoring students in the field of civil engineering, contributing to academic and practical advancements in engineering education.

'THANK YOU'